50 Lazy Fish Recipes

By: Kelly Johnson

Table of Contents

- Baked Lemon Garlic Salmon
- Tuna Salad Lettuce Wraps
- Fish Tacos (Bunless)
- Grilled Mahi-Mahi with Avocado Salsa
- Salmon Patties
- Simple Fish Stew
- Tuna Casserole
- Baked Cod with Dill and Lemon
- Shrimp and Avocado Salad
- Grilled Swordfish Steaks
- Fish and Chips (Keto-Style)
- Garlic Butter Shrimp Skillet
- Seared Tuna Steaks
- Fish Foil Packets
- Lemon Pepper Salmon
- Spicy Shrimp Stir Fry
- Grilled Salmon with Herb Butter

- Tuna-Stuffed Avocados
- Fish Chowder
- Smoked Salmon and Cream Cheese Roll-Ups
- Shrimp Scampi
- Shrimp and Broccoli Alfredo
- Grilled Trout with Herb Butter
- Fish Tacos with Cabbage Slaw
- Salmon Salad with Lemon Dressing
- Baked Tilapia with Garlic Butter
- Lemon Herb Fish Fillets
- Fish Fillet with Cilantro Lime Butter
- Shrimp and Cauliflower Grits
- Fish Stir Fry with Veggies
- Crispy Fish Fillets
- Sautéed Shrimp with Garlic
- Grilled Shrimp Skewers
- Lemon Garlic Butter Cod
- Salmon Cakes
- Shrimp Lettuce Wraps

- Baked Salmon with Mustard Sauce
- Fish Piccata
- Grilled Fish Tacos
- Shrimp and Zucchini Noodles
- Baked Cod with Parmesan Crust
- Baked Salmon with Pesto
- Seared Scallops with Garlic Butter
- Grilled Fish with Mango Salsa
- Prawn and Spinach Stir Fry
- Tuna Poke Bowl
- Shrimp and Asparagus Bake
- Lemon Dill Salmon
- Tuna Salad Cucumber Bites
- Grilled Halibut with Lemon Butter

Baked Lemon Garlic Salmon

Ingredients:

- 4 salmon fillets
- 2 tbsp olive oil
- 2 cloves garlic, minced
- 1 lemon, sliced
- Salt and pepper to taste
- Fresh parsley for garnish (optional)

Instructions:

1. Preheat oven to 375°F (190°C).
2. Place salmon fillets on a baking sheet lined with parchment paper.
3. Drizzle olive oil over the fillets, then sprinkle with minced garlic, salt, and pepper.
4. Place lemon slices on top of the fillets.
5. Bake for 15–20 minutes, or until salmon is cooked through and flakes easily with a fork.
6. Garnish with fresh parsley and serve.

Tuna Salad Lettuce Wraps

Ingredients:

- 1 can tuna, drained
- ¼ cup mayonnaise
- 1 tbsp Dijon mustard
- 1 tbsp lemon juice
- 1 stalk celery, chopped
- Salt and pepper to taste
- 4 large lettuce leaves (romaine or butter lettuce)

Instructions:

1. In a bowl, combine tuna, mayonnaise, mustard, lemon juice, celery, salt, and pepper.
2. Mix until well combined.
3. Spoon the tuna salad onto each lettuce leaf.
4. Wrap the lettuce around the tuna mixture and serve.

Fish Tacos (Bunless)

Ingredients:

- 4 small white fish fillets (tilapia, cod, etc.)
- 1 tbsp olive oil
- 1 tsp chili powder
- 1 tsp cumin
- 1 tsp garlic powder
- Salt and pepper to taste
- 1 avocado, sliced
- ½ cup shredded cabbage
- Fresh cilantro for garnish
- Lime wedges for serving

Instructions:

1. Preheat a grill or skillet over medium heat.
2. Season fish fillets with olive oil, chili powder, cumin, garlic powder, salt, and pepper.
3. Grill or cook fish for 3–4 minutes per side until cooked through.
4. Serve the fish on a bed of shredded cabbage, topped with avocado slices and fresh cilantro.
5. Garnish with lime wedges and serve.

Grilled Mahi-Mahi with Avocado Salsa

Ingredients:

- 4 mahi-mahi fillets
- 2 tbsp olive oil
- 1 tsp paprika
- 1 tsp garlic powder
- Salt and pepper to taste
- 1 avocado, diced
- 1 small tomato, diced
- ¼ red onion, diced
- 1 tbsp cilantro, chopped
- 1 tbsp lime juice

Instructions:

1. Preheat grill to medium-high heat.
2. Brush mahi-mahi fillets with olive oil and season with paprika, garlic powder, salt, and pepper.
3. Grill fish for 4–5 minutes per side until flaky and cooked through.
4. While the fish is grilling, combine avocado, tomato, onion, cilantro, and lime juice in a bowl to make the salsa.
5. Serve the grilled mahi-mahi topped with avocado salsa.

Salmon Patties

Ingredients:

- 1 can salmon, drained and flaked
- 1 egg, beaten
- ¼ cup almond flour
- 2 tbsp mayonnaise
- 1 tbsp Dijon mustard
- 1 tsp dried dill
- Salt and pepper to taste
- 2 tbsp olive oil for frying

Instructions:

1. In a bowl, mix together the salmon, egg, almond flour, mayonnaise, mustard, dill, salt, and pepper.
2. Form the mixture into 4–6 patties.
3. Heat olive oil in a skillet over medium heat.
4. Cook the patties for 3–4 minutes per side until golden brown and crispy.
5. Serve with a side of lemon wedges and fresh greens.

Simple Fish Stew

Ingredients:

- 1 lb white fish fillets (cod, tilapia, etc.), cut into chunks
- 2 tbsp olive oil
- 1 onion, chopped
- 2 cloves garlic, minced
- 2 cups fish stock or water
- 1 can diced tomatoes (no sugar added)
- 1 tsp smoked paprika
- 1 tsp thyme
- Salt and pepper to taste

Instructions:

1. Heat olive oil in a large pot over medium heat.
2. Add onion and garlic, cooking until softened.
3. Add fish stock, diced tomatoes, smoked paprika, thyme, salt, and pepper.
4. Bring to a simmer, then add fish chunks.
5. Simmer for 10–15 minutes until the fish is cooked through and the stew has thickened.
6. Serve hot with fresh herbs for garnish.

Tuna Casserole

Ingredients:

- 2 cans tuna, drained
- 1 cup cauliflower rice
- 1 cup shredded cheddar cheese
- ½ cup heavy cream
- 1 small onion, chopped
- 1 clove garlic, minced
- 1 tbsp olive oil
- Salt and pepper to taste
- 1 tsp dried parsley (optional)

Instructions:

1. Preheat oven to 375°F (190°C).
2. Sauté onion and garlic in olive oil until softened.
3. In a bowl, mix together the tuna, cauliflower rice, cheese, heavy cream, sautéed onion and garlic, salt, and pepper.
4. Pour the mixture into a casserole dish and bake for 20–25 minutes until bubbly and golden on top.
5. Garnish with parsley and serve.

Baked Cod with Dill and Lemon

Ingredients:

- 4 cod fillets
- 2 tbsp olive oil
- 1 lemon, sliced
- 2 tbsp fresh dill, chopped
- Salt and pepper to taste

Instructions:

1. Preheat oven to 375°F (190°C).
2. Place cod fillets on a baking sheet lined with parchment paper.
3. Drizzle with olive oil and season with salt, pepper, and fresh dill.
4. Place lemon slices on top of the fillets.
5. Bake for 12–15 minutes or until cod flakes easily with a fork.
6. Serve with extra lemon wedges for garnish.

Shrimp and Avocado Salad

Ingredients:

- 1 lb cooked shrimp, peeled and deveined
- 1 avocado, diced
- ½ cucumber, diced
- 1 tbsp olive oil
- 1 tbsp lime juice
- Salt and pepper to taste
- Fresh cilantro for garnish (optional)

Instructions:

1. In a bowl, combine shrimp, avocado, and cucumber.
2. Drizzle with olive oil and lime juice, then season with salt and pepper.
3. Toss to combine and garnish with fresh cilantro.
4. Serve chilled or at room temperature.

Grilled Swordfish Steaks

Ingredients:

- 4 swordfish steaks
- 2 tbsp olive oil
- 1 tbsp lemon juice
- 2 cloves garlic, minced
- 1 tsp dried oregano
- Salt and pepper to taste

Instructions:

1. Preheat grill to medium-high heat.
2. In a small bowl, mix olive oil, lemon juice, garlic, oregano, salt, and pepper.
3. Brush swordfish steaks with the marinade on both sides.
4. Grill the steaks for 4–5 minutes per side, or until they easily flake with a fork.
5. Serve immediately with a side of vegetables or a salad.

Fish and Chips (Keto-Style)

Ingredients:

- 4 white fish fillets (cod, haddock, or tilapia)
- 2 cups almond flour
- 1 tsp paprika
- 1 tsp garlic powder
- 1 tsp onion powder
- Salt and pepper to taste
- 2 eggs, beaten
- Olive oil for frying
- 2 large zucchinis, sliced into "fries"

Instructions:

1. Preheat oil in a skillet over medium-high heat for frying.
2. In a shallow bowl, combine almond flour, paprika, garlic powder, onion powder, salt, and pepper.
3. Dip each fish fillet into the beaten eggs, then coat in the almond flour mixture.
4. Fry the fish fillets in hot oil for 3–4 minutes per side until golden and crispy.
5. For the chips, toss zucchini slices in olive oil and season with salt. Roast at 400°F (200°C) for 15–20 minutes, turning halfway, until crispy.
6. Serve the fish with the zucchini fries and a squeeze of lemon.

Garlic Butter Shrimp Skillet

Ingredients:

- 1 lb large shrimp, peeled and deveined
- 3 tbsp butter
- 4 cloves garlic, minced
- 1 tbsp lemon juice
- Salt and pepper to taste
- Fresh parsley for garnish (optional)

Instructions:

1. Heat butter in a skillet over medium heat.
2. Add garlic and cook for 1-2 minutes until fragrant.
3. Add shrimp to the skillet, season with salt and pepper, and cook for 2-3 minutes per side until pink and cooked through.
4. Stir in lemon juice and cook for an additional minute.
5. Garnish with fresh parsley and serve.

Seared Tuna Steaks

Ingredients:

- 4 tuna steaks
- 2 tbsp olive oil
- 1 tbsp sesame oil
- Salt and pepper to taste
- 1 tbsp sesame seeds (optional)

Instructions:

1. Heat olive oil and sesame oil in a skillet over medium-high heat.
2. Season tuna steaks with salt and pepper on both sides.
3. Sear the tuna steaks for 1–2 minutes per side for rare, or longer if preferred.
4. If desired, sprinkle sesame seeds on the tuna steaks after searing.
5. Serve immediately with a fresh salad or roasted vegetables.

Fish Foil Packets

Ingredients:

- 4 white fish fillets (tilapia, cod, or similar)
- 1 lemon, thinly sliced
- 1 tbsp olive oil
- 2 cloves garlic, minced
- 2 tbsp fresh parsley, chopped
- Salt and pepper to taste

Instructions:

1. Preheat oven to 375°F (190°C).
2. Lay each fish fillet on a piece of aluminum foil.
3. Drizzle olive oil over the fish and sprinkle with garlic, salt, and pepper.
4. Top with lemon slices and fresh parsley.
5. Fold the foil over the fish to create a sealed packet.
6. Bake for 15–20 minutes until the fish is cooked through and flakes easily with a fork.
7. Serve the fish directly from the foil packets.

Lemon Pepper Salmon

Ingredients:

- 4 salmon fillets
- 2 tbsp olive oil
- 1 tbsp lemon juice
- 1 tsp lemon zest
- 1 tsp black pepper
- Salt to taste

Instructions:

1. Preheat oven to 375°F (190°C).
2. Place salmon fillets on a baking sheet lined with parchment paper.
3. Drizzle with olive oil and lemon juice, then sprinkle with lemon zest, black pepper, and salt.
4. Bake for 12–15 minutes, or until salmon flakes easily with a fork.
5. Serve with a side of steamed vegetables or a salad.

Spicy Shrimp Stir Fry

Ingredients:

- 1 lb shrimp, peeled and deveined
- 2 tbsp olive oil
- 1 red bell pepper, sliced
- 1 zucchini, sliced
- 1 tbsp soy sauce or coconut aminos
- 1 tsp chili flakes (or more for desired spice level)
- 2 cloves garlic, minced
- 1 tbsp sesame oil
- Fresh cilantro for garnish (optional)

Instructions:

1. Heat olive oil in a large skillet or wok over medium-high heat.
2. Add garlic and sauté for 1–2 minutes.
3. Add shrimp, red bell pepper, and zucchini, and cook for 3–4 minutes until shrimp are cooked through.
4. Stir in soy sauce or coconut aminos, chili flakes, and sesame oil.
5. Cook for an additional 1–2 minutes, then garnish with cilantro and serve.

Grilled Salmon with Herb Butter

Ingredients:

- 4 salmon fillets
- 2 tbsp olive oil
- 4 tbsp butter, softened
- 1 tbsp fresh dill, chopped
- 1 tbsp fresh parsley, chopped
- 1 tsp garlic powder
- Salt and pepper to taste

Instructions:

1. Preheat grill to medium-high heat.
2. Brush salmon fillets with olive oil and season with salt and pepper.
3. Grill the salmon for 4–5 minutes per side until it flakes easily.
4. In a small bowl, mix softened butter with dill, parsley, and garlic powder.
5. Serve the grilled salmon topped with the herb butter.

Tuna-Stuffed Avocados

Ingredients:

- 2 avocados, halved and pitted
- 1 can tuna, drained
- 2 tbsp mayonnaise
- 1 tbsp Dijon mustard
- 1 tbsp lemon juice
- Salt and pepper to taste

Instructions:

1. In a bowl, combine tuna, mayonnaise, Dijon mustard, lemon juice, salt, and pepper.
2. Scoop out a little of the avocado flesh to make space for the tuna mixture.
3. Stuff the avocado halves with the tuna salad.
4. Serve immediately with a sprinkle of fresh herbs, if desired.

Fish Chowder

Ingredients:

- 1 lb white fish fillets (cod, haddock, or similar), cut into chunks
- 2 tbsp butter
- 1 small onion, chopped
- 2 celery stalks, chopped
- 2 cloves garlic, minced
- 2 cups chicken or vegetable broth
- 1 cup heavy cream
- 1 tsp thyme
- Salt and pepper to taste

Instructions:

1. In a large pot, melt butter over medium heat.
2. Add onion, celery, and garlic and sauté for 5–7 minutes until softened.
3. Add broth, thyme, salt, and pepper. Bring to a simmer.
4. Stir in the fish and cook for 5–7 minutes until the fish is cooked through.
5. Stir in heavy cream and cook for an additional 2–3 minutes.
6. Serve hot, garnished with fresh herbs if desired.

Smoked Salmon and Cream Cheese Roll-Ups

Ingredients:

- 8 oz smoked salmon, sliced
- 4 oz cream cheese, softened
- 1 tbsp fresh dill, chopped
- 1 tbsp capers (optional)
- 1 tbsp lemon juice
- Fresh ground pepper to taste

Instructions:

1. Spread a thin layer of cream cheese on each slice of smoked salmon.
2. Sprinkle with chopped dill, capers (if using), and a squeeze of lemon juice.
3. Roll up each slice into a tight cylinder.
4. Garnish with a little fresh ground pepper and serve as a snack or appetizer.

Shrimp Scampi

Ingredients:

- 1 lb large shrimp, peeled and deveined
- 4 tbsp butter
- 4 cloves garlic, minced
- 1 tsp lemon juice
- 1 tsp red pepper flakes (optional)
- Salt and pepper to taste
- Fresh parsley, chopped, for garnish

Instructions:

1. Melt butter in a large skillet over medium heat.
2. Add garlic and cook for 1-2 minutes until fragrant.
3. Add shrimp and cook for 2-3 minutes per side, or until pink and cooked through.
4. Stir in lemon juice, red pepper flakes, salt, and pepper.
5. Garnish with fresh parsley and serve immediately with a side of veggies or cauliflower rice.

Shrimp and Broccoli Alfredo

Ingredients:

- 1 lb shrimp, peeled and deveined
- 2 cups broccoli florets
- 2 tbsp butter
- 1 cup heavy cream
- 1 cup grated Parmesan cheese
- 2 cloves garlic, minced
- Salt and pepper to taste

Instructions:

1. Steam or blanch the broccoli until tender, about 4–5 minutes.
2. In a large skillet, melt butter over medium heat and sauté garlic until fragrant.
3. Add shrimp to the skillet and cook for 2–3 minutes per side, until pink and cooked through.
4. Stir in heavy cream and bring to a simmer. Add Parmesan cheese and cook until the sauce thickens.
5. Season with salt and pepper, then toss in the cooked broccoli.
6. Serve immediately.

Grilled Trout with Herb Butter

Ingredients:

- 4 trout fillets
- 3 tbsp butter, softened
- 1 tbsp fresh parsley, chopped
- 1 tbsp fresh dill, chopped
- 1 tsp lemon zest
- Salt and pepper to taste

Instructions:

1. Preheat grill to medium-high heat.
2. Season trout fillets with salt and pepper.
3. In a small bowl, mix softened butter with parsley, dill, and lemon zest.
4. Grill trout fillets for 4–5 minutes per side, or until cooked through.
5. Top with herb butter before serving.

Fish Tacos with Cabbage Slaw

Ingredients:

- 4 white fish fillets (cod, tilapia, etc.)
- 2 tbsp olive oil
- 1 tsp chili powder
- 1 tsp cumin
- Salt and pepper to taste
- 1 cup shredded cabbage
- 2 tbsp mayonnaise
- 1 tbsp apple cider vinegar
- 1 tsp lime juice
- Fresh cilantro for garnish

Instructions:

1. Preheat grill or skillet to medium-high heat.
2. Season fish fillets with olive oil, chili powder, cumin, salt, and pepper.
3. Grill or pan-sear the fish for 3–4 minutes per side, or until cooked through.
4. In a bowl, combine shredded cabbage, mayonnaise, vinegar, and lime juice to make the slaw.
5. Serve the grilled fish with the cabbage slaw on top and garnish with fresh cilantro.

Salmon Salad with Lemon Dressing

Ingredients:

- 2 cups mixed greens
- 1 can (or 2 fillets) cooked salmon, flaked
- 1 avocado, diced
- 1 cucumber, sliced
- 1 tbsp olive oil
- 1 tbsp lemon juice
- Salt and pepper to taste

Instructions:

1. In a large bowl, toss mixed greens with avocado, cucumber, and flaked salmon.
2. In a small bowl, whisk together olive oil, lemon juice, salt, and pepper.
3. Drizzle the dressing over the salad and toss gently to coat.
4. Serve immediately.

Baked Tilapia with Garlic Butter

Ingredients:

- 4 tilapia fillets
- 4 tbsp butter, melted
- 3 cloves garlic, minced
- 1 tbsp fresh parsley, chopped
- 1 tbsp lemon juice
- Salt and pepper to taste

Instructions:

1. Preheat oven to 375°F (190°C).
2. Place tilapia fillets on a baking sheet lined with parchment paper.
3. In a small bowl, mix melted butter with garlic, parsley, lemon juice, salt, and pepper.
4. Pour the garlic butter over the tilapia fillets.
5. Bake for 12–15 minutes, or until the fish flakes easily with a fork.
6. Serve with a side of steamed vegetables.

Lemon Herb Fish Fillets

Ingredients:

- 4 white fish fillets (cod, haddock, etc.)
- 2 tbsp olive oil
- 1 lemon, sliced
- 1 tbsp fresh thyme, chopped
- 1 tbsp fresh parsley, chopped
- Salt and pepper to taste

Instructions:

1. Preheat oven to 400°F (200°C).
2. Place fish fillets on a baking sheet.
3. Drizzle with olive oil, and season with salt, pepper, thyme, and parsley.
4. Top with lemon slices.
5. Bake for 12–15 minutes or until the fish is cooked through and flakes easily.
6. Serve with extra lemon wedges and a fresh salad.

Fish Fillet with Cilantro Lime Butter

Ingredients:

- 4 fish fillets (tilapia, cod, or other white fish)
- 2 tbsp butter, softened
- 1 tbsp fresh cilantro, chopped
- 1 tbsp lime juice
- Salt and pepper to taste

Instructions:

1. Preheat grill or skillet to medium-high heat.
2. Season fish fillets with salt and pepper.
3. Grill or pan-sear the fish for 3–4 minutes per side, or until cooked through.
4. In a small bowl, mix softened butter with cilantro, lime juice, salt, and pepper.
5. Top the cooked fish with the cilantro lime butter before serving.

Shrimp and Cauliflower Grits

Ingredients:

- 1 lb shrimp, peeled and deveined
- 1 medium cauliflower, cut into florets
- 2 tbsp butter
- 1 cup heavy cream
- 1 cup chicken broth
- 2 cloves garlic, minced
- 1/4 cup grated Parmesan cheese
- Salt and pepper to taste
- Fresh parsley for garnish

Instructions:

1. Steam cauliflower florets until soft, about 10–12 minutes.
2. In a blender or food processor, blend the cauliflower with heavy cream and chicken broth until smooth.
3. Melt butter in a skillet over medium heat, add garlic, and sauté for 1–2 minutes.
4. Add shrimp to the skillet and cook for 3–4 minutes per side, until pink and cooked through.
5. Stir in Parmesan cheese, salt, and pepper, then add the cauliflower "grits."
6. Serve the shrimp on top of the cauliflower grits, garnished with fresh parsley.

Fish Stir Fry with Veggies

Ingredients:

- 1 lb white fish fillets (tilapia, cod, etc.), cut into chunks
- 2 tbsp olive oil
- 1 bell pepper, sliced
- 1 zucchini, sliced
- 1 cup snap peas
- 2 tbsp soy sauce or coconut aminos
- 2 cloves garlic, minced
- 1 tsp ginger, minced
- 1 tbsp sesame oil
- Fresh cilantro for garnish

Instructions:

1. Heat olive oil in a large skillet over medium-high heat.
2. Add fish chunks and cook for 2–3 minutes per side, until golden brown. Remove and set aside.
3. In the same skillet, add bell pepper, zucchini, and snap peas. Sauté for 4–5 minutes until tender.
4. Stir in garlic, ginger, soy sauce (or coconut aminos), and sesame oil. Cook for 2 minutes.
5. Add the cooked fish back into the skillet and toss to combine.

6. Garnish with fresh cilantro and serve.

Crispy Fish Fillets

Ingredients:

- 4 white fish fillets (cod, haddock, etc.)
- 1 cup almond flour
- 1/2 cup grated Parmesan cheese
- 1 tsp garlic powder
- 1 tsp onion powder
- 1/2 tsp paprika
- 2 eggs, beaten
- Salt and pepper to taste
- Olive oil for frying

Instructions:

1. In a shallow bowl, combine almond flour, Parmesan, garlic powder, onion powder, paprika, salt, and pepper.
2. Dip each fish fillet into the beaten eggs, then coat in the almond flour mixture.
3. Heat olive oil in a skillet over medium heat. Fry the fish for 3–4 minutes per side, until golden and crispy.
4. Serve with a side of veggies or a fresh salad.

Sautéed Shrimp with Garlic

Ingredients:

- 1 lb shrimp, peeled and deveined
- 2 tbsp butter
- 4 cloves garlic, minced
- 1 tbsp lemon juice
- Salt and pepper to taste
- Fresh parsley for garnish

Instructions:

1. Melt butter in a large skillet over medium heat.
2. Add garlic and cook for 1–2 minutes, until fragrant.
3. Add shrimp to the skillet and cook for 2–3 minutes per side, until pink and cooked through.
4. Stir in lemon juice, salt, and pepper.
5. Garnish with fresh parsley and serve immediately.

Grilled Shrimp Skewers

Ingredients:

- 1 lb large shrimp, peeled and deveined
- 2 tbsp olive oil
- 1 tbsp lemon juice
- 2 cloves garlic, minced
- 1 tsp smoked paprika
- 1 tsp dried oregano
- Salt and pepper to taste
- Skewers (wooden or metal)

Instructions:

1. Preheat grill to medium-high heat.
2. In a bowl, mix olive oil, lemon juice, garlic, paprika, oregano, salt, and pepper.
3. Thread shrimp onto skewers. Brush the shrimp with the marinade.
4. Grill shrimp for 2–3 minutes per side, or until pink and cooked through.
5. Serve with a side of veggies or salad.

Lemon Garlic Butter Cod

Ingredients:

- 4 cod fillets
- 4 tbsp butter
- 2 cloves garlic, minced
- 1 tbsp lemon juice
- Salt and pepper to taste
- Fresh parsley for garnish

Instructions:

1. Preheat oven to 375°F (190°C).
2. Place cod fillets on a baking sheet lined with parchment paper.
3. In a small saucepan, melt butter over medium heat. Add garlic and sauté for 1–2 minutes until fragrant.
4. Stir in lemon juice, salt, and pepper.
5. Pour the garlic butter mixture over the cod fillets.
6. Bake for 12–15 minutes, or until the fish flakes easily with a fork.
7. Garnish with fresh parsley and serve.

Salmon Cakes

Ingredients:

- 2 cans (6 oz each) pink salmon, drained and flaked
- 1 egg
- 1/4 cup almond flour
- 1 tbsp Dijon mustard
- 1 tbsp fresh parsley, chopped
- 1 tsp garlic powder
- Salt and pepper to taste
- 2 tbsp olive oil for frying

Instructions:

1. In a bowl, combine salmon, egg, almond flour, mustard, parsley, garlic powder, salt, and pepper. Mix until well combined.
2. Form the mixture into patties.
3. Heat olive oil in a skillet over medium heat. Fry the salmon cakes for 3–4 minutes per side, until golden and crispy.
4. Serve with a side of veggies or a dipping sauce.

Shrimp Lettuce Wraps

Ingredients:

- 1 lb shrimp, peeled and deveined
- 2 tbsp olive oil
- 2 tbsp lime juice
- 1 tsp chili powder
- Salt and pepper to taste
- 1 head of lettuce (such as iceberg or butterhead), leaves separated
- 1/4 cup avocado, diced
- 1/4 cup shredded carrots
- Fresh cilantro for garnish

Instructions:

1. Heat olive oil in a skillet over medium heat.
2. Add shrimp and cook for 2-3 minutes per side until pink and cooked through.
3. Stir in lime juice, chili powder, salt, and pepper.
4. Place cooked shrimp in lettuce leaves, and top with diced avocado, shredded carrots, and fresh cilantro.
5. Serve immediately.

Baked Salmon with Mustard Sauce

Ingredients:

- 4 salmon fillets
- 2 tbsp Dijon mustard
- 1 tbsp honey (optional, for a touch of sweetness)
- 1 tbsp olive oil
- 1 tbsp lemon juice
- Salt and pepper to taste
- Fresh dill for garnish

Instructions:

1. Preheat oven to 375°F (190°C).
2. Place salmon fillets on a baking sheet lined with parchment paper.
3. In a small bowl, mix Dijon mustard, honey, olive oil, lemon juice, salt, and pepper.
4. Spread the mustard sauce over the top of each salmon fillet.
5. Bake for 12–15 minutes, or until the salmon is cooked through and flakes easily with a fork.
6. Garnish with fresh dill and serve.

Fish Piccata

Ingredients:

- 4 white fish fillets (cod, tilapia, or halibut)
- 2 tbsp olive oil
- 1/4 cup almond flour
- 2 tbsp butter
- 2 cloves garlic, minced
- 1/4 cup capers
- 1/4 cup lemon juice
- 1/4 cup chicken broth
- Fresh parsley, chopped for garnish
- Salt and pepper to taste

Instructions:

1. Season the fish fillets with salt and pepper, then dredge in almond flour.

2. Heat olive oil in a skillet over medium-high heat. Add the fish and cook for 3–4 minutes per side, until golden brown and cooked through. Remove the fish from the skillet.

3. In the same skillet, melt butter and sauté garlic for 1 minute.

4. Add capers, lemon juice, and chicken broth, then cook for 2–3 minutes to allow the sauce to thicken slightly.

5. Return the fish to the skillet and spoon the sauce over the fillets.

6. Garnish with fresh parsley and serve.

Grilled Fish Tacos

Ingredients:

- 4 white fish fillets (cod, tilapia, or mahi-mahi)
- 1 tbsp olive oil
- 1 tsp cumin
- 1 tsp chili powder
- 1/2 tsp paprika
- Salt and pepper to taste
- 1 cup cabbage, shredded
- 1 tbsp lime juice
- 1 avocado, sliced
- Fresh cilantro for garnish
- Low-carb tortillas or lettuce wraps for serving

Instructions:

1. Preheat grill to medium-high heat.
2. Rub fish fillets with olive oil, cumin, chili powder, paprika, salt, and pepper.
3. Grill fish for 3–4 minutes per side, until cooked through and easily flaked.
4. In a small bowl, toss shredded cabbage with lime juice.
5. To assemble, place the grilled fish in tortillas or lettuce wraps, top with cabbage, avocado slices, and fresh cilantro.

6. Serve with a side of lime wedges.

Shrimp and Zucchini Noodles

Ingredients:

- 1 lb shrimp, peeled and deveined
- 2 medium zucchinis, spiralized into noodles
- 2 tbsp olive oil
- 2 cloves garlic, minced
- 1/2 tsp red pepper flakes (optional)
- 1/4 cup chicken broth
- 1/4 cup Parmesan cheese, grated
- Salt and pepper to taste
- Fresh parsley for garnish

Instructions:

1. Heat olive oil in a skillet over medium heat. Add garlic and cook for 1-2 minutes until fragrant.
2. Add shrimp to the skillet and cook for 2-3 minutes per side until pink and cooked through. Remove shrimp and set aside.
3. In the same skillet, add chicken broth and zucchini noodles. Sauté for 2-3 minutes until the noodles are tender but still al dente.
4. Return shrimp to the skillet and toss with the zucchini noodles.
5. Stir in Parmesan cheese and season with salt and pepper.
6. Garnish with fresh parsley and serve.

Baked Cod with Parmesan Crust

Ingredients:

- 4 cod fillets
- 1/2 cup grated Parmesan cheese
- 1/4 cup almond flour
- 1 tbsp parsley, chopped
- 1 tbsp garlic powder
- 2 tbsp butter, melted
- Salt and pepper to taste

Instructions:

1. Preheat oven to 400°F (200°C).
2. In a bowl, mix Parmesan cheese, almond flour, parsley, garlic powder, salt, and pepper.
3. Place cod fillets on a baking sheet lined with parchment paper. Brush fillets with melted butter.
4. Coat each fillet with the Parmesan mixture, pressing lightly to adhere.
5. Bake for 12–15 minutes, or until the fish flakes easily with a fork and the crust is golden brown.
6. Serve with a side of sautéed vegetables.

Baked Salmon with Pesto

Ingredients:

- 4 salmon fillets
- 1/2 cup pesto (store-bought or homemade)
- 1 tbsp olive oil
- Salt and pepper to taste
- Fresh basil for garnish

Instructions:

1. Preheat oven to 375°F (190°C).
2. Place salmon fillets on a baking sheet lined with parchment paper.
3. Drizzle with olive oil and season with salt and pepper.
4. Spoon pesto over each fillet.
5. Bake for 12–15 minutes, or until the salmon is cooked through and flakes easily.
6. Garnish with fresh basil and serve.

Seared Scallops with Garlic Butter

Ingredients:

- 1 lb sea scallops, patted dry
- 2 tbsp butter
- 2 cloves garlic, minced
- 1 tbsp fresh parsley, chopped
- 1 tbsp lemon juice
- Salt and pepper to taste

Instructions:

1. Heat butter in a large skillet over medium-high heat.
2. Season scallops with salt and pepper.
3. Once the butter is melted and bubbling, add the scallops to the skillet and cook for 2–3 minutes per side, until golden brown and cooked through.
4. Add garlic and cook for 30 seconds, until fragrant.
5. Stir in lemon juice and fresh parsley.
6. Serve immediately, garnished with extra parsley.

Grilled Fish with Mango Salsa

Ingredients:

- 4 white fish fillets (tilapia, cod, or mahi-mahi)
- 1 tbsp olive oil
- Salt and pepper to taste
- 1 mango, diced
- 1/2 red onion, finely diced
- 1/2 cup cilantro, chopped
- 1 tbsp lime juice
- 1/2 jalapeño, diced (optional)

Instructions:

1. Preheat grill to medium-high heat.
2. Brush the fish fillets with olive oil and season with salt and pepper.
3. Grill fish for 3–4 minutes per side, or until cooked through.
4. In a bowl, combine diced mango, red onion, cilantro, lime juice, and jalapeño (if using).
5. Serve the grilled fish topped with the mango salsa.

Prawn and Spinach Stir Fry

Ingredients:

- 1 lb prawns, peeled and deveined
- 2 cups spinach, fresh
- 2 tbsp olive oil
- 2 cloves garlic, minced
- 1/2 tsp red pepper flakes (optional)
- 2 tbsp soy sauce or coconut aminos
- 1 tbsp sesame oil
- Salt and pepper to taste
- Sesame seeds for garnish

Instructions:

1. Heat olive oil in a large skillet or wok over medium-high heat.
2. Add garlic and red pepper flakes (if using), and sauté for 1–2 minutes.
3. Add prawns to the skillet and cook for 2–3 minutes per side, until they turn pink and are cooked through.
4. Stir in spinach and cook for another 1–2 minutes, until wilted.
5. Add soy sauce (or coconut aminos) and sesame oil, tossing to coat.
6. Season with salt and pepper to taste.
7. Garnish with sesame seeds and serve.

Tuna Poke Bowl

Ingredients:

- 1 lb fresh tuna, diced into cubes
- 1 tbsp sesame oil
- 1 tbsp soy sauce or coconut aminos
- 1/2 tsp rice vinegar
- 1/2 tsp honey (optional)
- 1/4 cup cucumber, diced
- 1/4 cup avocado, diced
- 1/4 cup radishes, sliced
- 1/4 cup edamame (optional)
- 1 tbsp sesame seeds
- Seaweed salad (optional)
- Fresh cilantro for garnish

Instructions:

1. In a bowl, combine tuna, sesame oil, soy sauce (or coconut aminos), rice vinegar, and honey (if using). Toss to coat the tuna evenly and refrigerate for 10–15 minutes to marinate.
2. To assemble the poke bowl, place the marinated tuna in the center of a bowl.
3. Arrange cucumber, avocado, radishes, edamame, and seaweed salad (if using) around the tuna.

4. Sprinkle with sesame seeds and garnish with fresh cilantro.

5. Serve immediately.

Shrimp and Asparagus Bake

Ingredients:

- 1 lb shrimp, peeled and deveined
- 1 bunch asparagus, trimmed and cut into 2-inch pieces
- 2 tbsp olive oil
- 2 cloves garlic, minced
- 1 tsp paprika
- 1 tsp lemon zest
- Salt and pepper to taste
- 1 tbsp fresh parsley, chopped

Instructions:

1. Preheat oven to 400°F (200°C).
2. In a bowl, toss shrimp and asparagus with olive oil, garlic, paprika, lemon zest, salt, and pepper.
3. Spread the mixture evenly on a baking sheet.
4. Bake for 12–15 minutes, until the shrimp is pink and cooked through, and the asparagus is tender.
5. Garnish with fresh parsley and serve immediately.

Lemon Dill Salmon

Ingredients:

- 4 salmon fillets
- 2 tbsp olive oil
- 2 tbsp fresh dill, chopped
- 1 tbsp lemon juice
- 1 tsp lemon zest
- Salt and pepper to taste
- Lemon slices for garnish

Instructions:

1. Preheat oven to 375°F (190°C).
2. Place salmon fillets on a baking sheet lined with parchment paper.
3. Drizzle olive oil over the fillets, then sprinkle with chopped dill, lemon juice, lemon zest, salt, and pepper.
4. Bake for 12–15 minutes, or until the salmon is cooked through and flakes easily with a fork.
5. Garnish with lemon slices and serve.

Tuna Salad Cucumber Bites

Ingredients:

- 1 can (5 oz) tuna in water, drained
- 1/4 cup mayonnaise
- 1 tbsp Dijon mustard
- 1/2 tbsp lemon juice
- 1/4 tsp garlic powder
- Salt and pepper to taste
- 1 cucumber, sliced into rounds
- Fresh parsley for garnish

Instructions:

1. In a bowl, mix together tuna, mayonnaise, Dijon mustard, lemon juice, garlic powder, salt, and pepper.
2. Arrange cucumber slices on a serving platter.
3. Spoon the tuna salad mixture onto each cucumber round.
4. Garnish with fresh parsley and serve immediately.

Grilled Halibut with Lemon Butter

Ingredients:

- 4 halibut fillets
- 2 tbsp olive oil
- 1 tbsp lemon juice
- 2 tbsp butter, melted
- 1 tsp garlic powder
- Salt and pepper to taste
- Fresh parsley for garnish
- Lemon wedges for serving

Instructions:

1. Preheat grill to medium-high heat.
2. Brush halibut fillets with olive oil and season with salt, pepper, and garlic powder.
3. Grill the halibut for 4–5 minutes per side, until the fish is opaque and flakes easily with a fork.
4. In a small bowl, mix together melted butter and lemon juice.
5. Drizzle the lemon butter over the grilled halibut and garnish with fresh parsley.
6. Serve with lemon wedges on the side.